To Ingrid
My sister in C[...]
May our Lord [...]
bless you.
Love in Jesus
June

Also by Selwyn Hughes
in this series
The Divine Eagle
The Divine Gardener

THE
DIVINE
ATTITUDES

Key qualities for effective living

SELWYN HUGHES

Illustrated by Brian Norwood

© CWR 1989

CWR, 10 Brooklands Close,
Sunbury-on-Thames, Middx TW16 7DX

NATIONAL DISTRIBUTORS
Australia: Christian Marketing Pty Ltd., PO Box 154, North Geelong,
Victoria 3215   Tel: (052) 786100
Canada: Canadian Christian Distributors Inc., PO Box 550, Virgil,
Ontario LOS 1TO   Tel: 416 641 0631
Republic of Ireland: Merrion Press Ltd, 10 D'Olier Street, Dublin
Tel & Fax 773316
Malaysia: Salvation Book Centre, (M) Sdn. Bhd., 23 Jalan SS2/64,
47300 Petaling Jaya, Selangor
New Zealand: CWR (NZ), PO Box 4108, Mount Maunganui 3030
Tel: (075) 757412
Singapore: Alby Commercial Enterprises Pte Ltd., Garden Hotel,
14 Balmoral Road, Singapore 1025
Southern Africa: CWR (Southern Africa), PO Box 43 Kenilworth, 7745, RSA
Tel: (021) 7612560

Typeset by Watermark, Watford

Printed in Great Britain by
BPCC Paulton Books Limited

ISBN 1–85345–032–4 Hardback
ISBN 1–85345–033–2 Limp
First published 1986 and reprinted in illustrated format 1989

INTRODUCTION

Ever since I came across them in the early days of my Christian experience, the Beatitudes – the eight sayings of Jesus which preface His Sermon on the Mount – have been for me a source of deep interest and fascination.

At first I considered them to be a little idealistic – great words to repeat or recite but beyond the ability of man to continually practise. Then I discovered the powerful spiritual principle that applies not just to the Sermon on the Mount but to every part of the Bible: God does more than lift the standards to almost unbelievable heights – He also provides the power by which we can reach up to them. When one is surrendered to Him, then "nothing is impossible".

Each one of these eight statements of Jesus contains the spiritual motivation to change and transform our every attitude – if we let them. Over the past two thousand years they have been altering the moods and minds of multitudes of men and women. Thus they have passed many tests, including the test of time. I have no hesitation in saying that they have been the spirit that has driven my own life for close on four decades. My prayer is that as you come in touch with them a whole new world will open up to your consciousness and that you will discover, as millions of others have done, God's blueprint for successful and effective living.

Selwyn Hughes

BLESSED ARE ...

One of the most powerful and profound passages in Scripture is that known as *the Beatitudes*.

Matthew 5:1–11

We must begin studying the Beatitudes by laying down the thought that the eight principles which comprise the Beatitudes are the *best prescription for mental and spiritual health it is possible to find.* Dr James Fisher, a well-known and widely travelled psychiatrist, went throughout the world looking for the positive qualities that make for good mental health. He said: "I dreamed of writing a handbook that would be simple, practical, easy to understand and easy to follow; it would tell people how to live – what thoughts and attitudes and philosophies to cultivate, and what pitfalls to avoid in seeking mental health. And quite by accident I discovered that such a work had been completed – the Beatitudes."

What an amazing admission! I would go as far as to say that once a person absorbs the principles which underlie the Beatitudes – and lives by them – then that person will never again fall prey to serious depression or despair. How sad that so often the Christian Church has to refer its depressed and discouraged people to the mental experts of the world when we hold in our hands the blueprint for healthy and abundant living.

Dr Raymond Cramer, a minister and a Christian psychologist, describes the Beatitudes as "the psychology of Jesus". Some may find that expression unacceptable when applied to the Beatitudes, but remember, this is a scientist who is speaking. In studying the laws of human behaviour and seeking to discover what it is that brings a person to his highest

point of integration, he came to see that the words of Jesus in the Beatitudes reveal more succinctly and more clearly than any other section of literature the principles by which a person can know contentment and inner happiness. In an age which is fascinated with the study of human behaviour, there is only one true psychology – the psychology of Jesus.

John 2:12–25

v. 25

It is helpful to keep in mind that the Beatitudes are *be*-attitudes, not *do*-attitudes; the doing comes out of the being. Some ministers and commentators refer to them as 'the beautiful attitudes' – a phrase I find greatly appealing.

Romans 13:7–14

v. 14

Our attitudes have a tremendous and powerful influence upon every part of our being – physical as well as emotional. A missionary from the Philippines tells

how, during the war, he and his wife were ordered into prison camps by the Japanese, and were instructed that they could take with them all they could carry in their suitcases and no more. His wife, weighing just over 100 pounds, and not at all strong, carried a load of 200 pounds, mostly tinned food, a distance of five miles – a load neither of them could even lift after they arrived.

Mannheim, a famous scientist, says that we normally use about one-eighth of our physical reserves, and that these reserves are only called upon when we employ the right attitudes. If our attitudes can help tap hidden physical reserves, then think of what our experience can be if we adopt the 'beautiful attitudes' which our Lord expounds for us in His Sermon on the Mount. We can maximise our potential and multiply our effectiveness,

not only in the physical area of our being, but in our mental and emotional areas also. Many doctors and scientists agree that it is not our arteries but our attitudes which have the biggest say in our personal well-being.

According to an article in the British Medical Journal, "there is not a tissue or organ in the body that is not influenced by the attitude of mind and spirit". Dr Frank Hutchins, a nerve specialist, said: "Seventy per cent of the medical cases I see need new mental and spiritual attitudes for health." Man is a unit made up of spirit, soul and body, and he cannot be sick in one part without passing on the sickness to other parts. The attitudes we hold in our minds do not stay merely as attitudes – they pass over into definite physical effects.

1 Corinthians 6:12–20
v. 19

God has so designed our beings that the right attitudes produce the right effects in our bodies. Suppose they produced the wrong effects? Then the body and morality would be alien to one another. An outstanding surgeon said: "I've discovered the kingdom of God at the end of my scalpel; it's in the tissues. The right thing morally is always the right thing physically." The laws of morality and the laws of health are written by the same God for the same purpose – healthy and happy living.

The greatest source of power for physical health is the absence of inward clash and strife in the spirit. Many people could be well physically if they were well spiritually. Other things being equal, a Christian should be healthier and happier than a non-Christian, for he or she has access to the attitudes that contribute to health.

We have seen that God has designed our beings in such a way that right attitudes in the mind produce right effects in the body. William James says: "The greatest revolution in my generation was the discovery that human beings, by changing their inner attitudes of mind, could alter the outer aspects of their lives." We could say that any results in life, any evidence of good mental health (and perhaps even physical health), any spiritual growth and maturity hinge on our understanding of the truths which our Lord expounds for us in the Beatitudes. They are the gateway to health and happiness. Let's decide here and now that no matter how much effort we have to make to understand and absorb these powerful and important principles, we will not give up until they become part of our daily thinking and our daily living.

Jeremiah
17:5–14
vv. 7–8

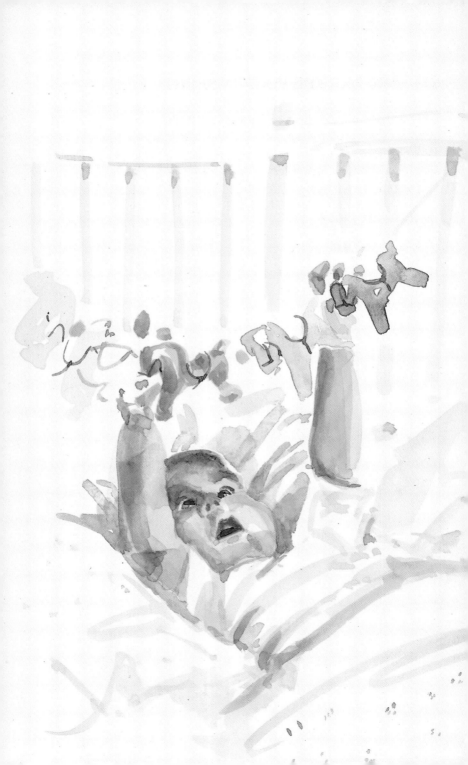

BLESSED ARE THE POOR IN SPIRIT

When we understand the fact that the Beatitudes provide us with the right mental and spiritual attitudes we are ready to focus on the first of these profound statements of our Lord: "Blessed are the poor in spirit, for theirs is the kingdom of heaven."

Some translations read, *"Happy* are the poor in spirit...", and one goes as far as to say, *"Congratulations* to the poor in spirit..." It is important to keep in mind as you go through the Beatitudes that the word 'happy' (Greek: *makarios*) carries a far richer tone than we commonly attach to the word. It suggests a deep, abiding happiness, not just a temporary emotional lift.

1 Thessalonians 5:12–24

v. 16

In the very first words of the Sermon on the Mount, therefore, Jesus puts His finger on one of life's most vital issues – individual and personal happiness. We all want to be happy – and rightly so. The longing for deep, lasting happiness is a deep-rooted instinct that has been built into us by the Creator Himself. The God who made the sunset, painted the rose, put the smile on a baby's face, gave the gift of playfulness to a kitten and put laughter in our souls is surely not happy when we are unhappy. The universe is on the side of the old saying that goes: "Down with the coffee-pot face, up with the teapot face."

Although it is a God-given instinct to be happy, we must also see that it is only God who can make us happy. Apart from Him and His redemptive love as expressed through the cross and the resurrection, we would be 'most miserable' (1 Cor.15:19). As someone once put it: "Now that I know Christ, I'm happier when I'm sad than before when I was glad."

1 Corinthians 15:19

But happiness is not something you *make* but something you *receive*. In Mark 6:48, it is said that the Mark 6:45–51
v. 48 disciples were toiling, rowing in the dark and getting nowhere. The wind and the waves were against them and the whole thing was ending in futility. Then Jesus came. In John's account of the same event, we are told that they took Him into their boat and immediately – the boat was at the land where they were going (John 6:21). John 6:21 This is the way it is with happiness. We strive to achieve it, but we 'toil in rowing'. Then we let Christ in – and lo, we are at the land where we were going.

If happiness is not something we can create but something we receive, how do we go about receiving it? Listen again to the words of Jesus: "Blessed are the poor

in spirit, for theirs is the kingdom of heaven."

What does it mean to be 'poor in spirit'? There are those who tell us that the words should read, "Blessed in spirit are the poor" – an idea derived from Luke 6:20, which reads: "Blessed are you who are poor, for yours is the kingdom of God." Our Lord, however, is not thinking here of material poverty, but spiritual poverty: "Blessed are the poor *in spirit*". The word for 'poor' in the Greek is *ptochos* and means a chosen poverty. It implies a voluntary emptying of the inner being and refers to those who by choice are so poor that they become poor enough to receive. One translation puts it: "Blessed are those who are receptive in spirit" – those who are willing to empty their hands of their own

Luke 6:20

Mark 10:13–31
v. 15

possessions and have them filled with the riches of God.

Jesus' first prescription for happiness, then, is a voluntary act of self-renunciation. This reverses the usual prescriptions for happiness, which begin with words such as 'assert', 'take', 'release' or 'affirm'. Which prescription will the universe back? I have no doubt myself – it is the prescription of Jesus. The first step, then, toward mental and spiritual health is self-renunciation. It is the decision we must take to reach out and receive Christ – with empty hands. Note that – *with empty hands.* The reason why so many fail to find Christ is because they are unreceptive – Christ cannot give Himself to them because they do not give themselves to Him.

When we are willing to acknowledge our need of Christ and stop striving to find happiness but receive Him into our lives – then lo, like the disciples, we have reached the land where we were going.

It ought not to be considered strange that the entrance into the kingdom of God begins in receptivity – isn't that where all life begins? Our scientists tell us that the ovum and the sperm have to receive each other before they can begin the positive business of producing active life. The seed in the ground receives moisture and nutrition from the earth before it can begin to give forth in flower and fruit. If it doesn't begin with receptivity, it doesn't begin. The scientist who does not sit down before the facts as a little child and who is not prepared to give up every preconceived notion and follow to whatever end nature will lead him will know nothing. He has to know that he doesn't know in order to know.

The first law of life is receptivity, and that is also the first law of the kingdom of God. Look at John 1:12: "As

John 1:1–14

v. 12

many as received him, to them gave he power to become the sons of God". How do we get power? First by receptivity – "as many as received him". At the very threshold of Christ's kingdom, then, we are met with the demand for self-emptying and receptivity. Have you made your own personal response to this demand? If not, I urge you to do it today. If you are not willing to do this, then nothing else can follow – if you are willing, then everything else follows.

The plain truth of what Christ is saying, then, in the words, "Blessed (or happy) are the poor in spirit", is that we must choose to give up whatever we are holding and allow Him to fill our lives with His forgiveness, love and

power. A highly cultured and beautiful woman, after reviewing her life, said with a sigh: "I have everything – and nothing." Everything in the way of comforts and riches – yet empty in heart. To find happiness, we must find Christ. And how do we find Him? We do what Bartimaeus did (Mark 10:50) – fling away our 'cloak' and run to Jesus.

Mark 10:46–52
v. 50

Luke tells us how on one occasion as Jesus passed along the road, a multitude thronged around Him. A woman in deep need came timidly through the crowd and touched His garment. "Who touched me?" asked Jesus as He felt power go forth from Him. The disciples replied: "Master, the multitudes throng you, so why do

Luke 8:40–56
v. 44

you say, 'Who touched me?'" "Somebody *touched* me", said Jesus. He knew that there was a great difference between thronging Him and touching Him. Those who throng Jesus get little, those who touch Jesus get everything.

Sunday after Sunday, thousands of people go to church and listen; they throng Jesus but never touch Him. Perhaps you are one. Some go to church for a lifetime and never really touch Him. If you are one of those people who constantly throng Jesus but never touch Him, then I pray that as you meditate on the opening words of the Beatitudes, you will reach out and touch Christ in a definite and personal way. Touch Him now – today – touch Him for forgiveness, for cleansing, for power over temptation, over fears, over anxieties, over everything that stands in the way of your personal happiness. As Christ gave Himself to those who needed Him when He was here on earth, so He does today. Cease thronging Him – touch Him.

When our Lord was here on earth, everyone needed Him, but only those who realised their need got His attention. It is often said that God rushes to the side of a person in need. That is not quite true. It would be more correct to say – *God rushes to the side of the person who recognises and acknowledges their need.* Those who recognise their need are to be congratulated, they are to be envied – they are candidates for the kingdom of heaven.

We could almost translate this first Beatitude in the following manner without doing any injustice to the original statement of Jesus: "Congratulations to those who are humble and willing enough to recognise their need – for then they are candidates for the help of God."

Luke 19: 1–10
v. 10

Take it from me, there is no one in the kingdom of God who is not 'poor in spirit'. You cannot be filled until first you are empty. Salvation is not something earned, but something received. It is by grace we are saved, through faith, and that not of ourselves, it is the gift of God (Eph. 2:8). The old hymn puts it in a way that is powerful and effective.

Ephesians 2:8

> "Nothing in my hand I bring,
> Simply to thy cross I cling...
> Foul, I to the fountain fly;
> Wash me, Saviour, or I die."

BLESSED ARE THOSE WHO MOURN

We turn now to consider the second of our Lord's Beatitudes: "Blessed are those who mourn, for they will be comforted." It is important to note that there is a very definite order in these sayings of Christ. Our Lord does not present them in a haphazard or accidental manner. Every one is carefully thought out and is given a precise and proper place in the spiritual sequence. Once we see that the entrance into the kingdom of God is through the acknowledgement of one's spiritual poverty and the acceptance of Christ's riches and resources, we are then ready to consider the next: "Happy are those who know what sorrow means, for they will be given courage and comfort" (J.B.Phillips).

'Those who mourn' – the word 'mourn' has reference to more than just sorrowing over the death of a loved one – it includes all those experiences in life where we may feel crushed, broken or sorrowful. I feel the best translation of this verse is the one given by J.B. Phillips which I quote again: "Happy are those who know what sorrow means, for they will be given courage and comfort."

Why should people who are caught up in the throes of distressing and sorrowful experiences be congratulated? The conclusion of the verse gives the answer – "**for they will be comforted**". And what then? Out of the comfort they receive, they are able to give comfort to others. Examine 2 Corinthians 1:3–4 in your Bible or listen to it as J.B.Phillips paraphrases it: "For he gives us comfort

2 Corinthians
1:1–11

in all our trials so that we in turn may be able to give the same sort of strong sympathy to others in their troubles."

vv. 3–4

I cannot think of anything more psychologically in harmony with the best thinking of today's social scientists than the words of Jesus in the second Beatitude. We would not be taking any undue liberty with the text of Matthew 5:4 if we translated it thus: "Congratulations to those who are willing to face and feel sorrow, for they will discover in and through the comfort that I impart to them a new ministry and a new joy."

Matthew 5:4

A mentally and spiritually healthy person is someone who is willing to face and feel sorrow, and recognise that it can be made to deepen one's life – not devastate it. You are familiar, I am sure, with the terms 'neurotic' and 'psychotic'. They are words used by the mental health experts of our day to describe certain attitudes and certain psychological conditions. A 'neurotic' is someone who is afraid to face reality, while a 'psychotic' is someone who is unaware of reality.

Psalm 51:1–12 v. 6

If we draw back from being willing to face and feel any emotion that rises up within us, then the denial of this feeling will have negative results within our personality. A woman once said to me: "I have problems with the second Beatitude because I don't know how to mourn; I am too happy to mourn." As we talked, it became clear to her that it wasn't so much that she didn't know how to mourn, but that she didn't *want* to mourn. She was afraid to face or feel any negative emotions – grief, sorrow, etc. – and thus, despite her claim to happiness and lightheartedness, she was a stunted soul. Whenever we are unwilling to face a negative emotion that reverberates within us, it implies that we are not in control of it, but that it is in control of us.

Christians are often taught to pretend that they feel joyful and happy when really they are miserable. The letter to the Hebrews, however, tells us that we have a great High Priest who can sympathise with us in our *weaknesses*. How pointless and purposeless it is to conceal our weaknesses from the Lord and deny ourselves the comfort of His uncritical and compassionate understanding. This is terribly important, for in my experience I would say that eight out of ten Christians have a completely wrong view of

Hebrews
4:12–16
v. 15

how to handle the hurts and sorrows that come into their lives.

The typical Christian reaction to negative emotions is either denial or expression. While denial is refusing to *face* them and *feel* them – often leading to psychosomatic disorders – expression of emotions is the act of letting our emotions out. This is a popular approach with many of today's counsellors and therapists. They say when you feel upset, hurt or angry, then shout and scream or punch a pillow until you have released those pent-up emotions. There is no doubt that some relief can be gained in this way, but the right way

of handling negative feelings is neither to deny them or express them, but to acknowledge them.

Neither denial nor expression, in my view, is a Biblical way of dealing with negative emotions. In fact, a recent research by some psychologists shows that the uncontrolled expression of negative feelings can compound, rather than clear up, one's emotional difficulties.

In my judgment, the correct and Biblical way to handle negative emotions is to acknowledge them fully before God and share with Him how we feel. Now understand clearly what I am saying, for at this point many have responded to this advice by coming to God when they are hurt or sorrowful and saying: "Lord, please forgive me for feeling hurt." That misses the point entirely. A Christian psychologist puts the issue most effectively when he says: "We are not to pretend that we feel *penitent* when we feel *hurt.*"

Psalm
139:1–24
v. 23

When our stomachs are churning with grief, sorrow or hurt, we must come before the One who sees and knows everything, and pray a prayer something like this: "Lord, right now I am hurting more than I think I can endure. I feel like screaming, running away or hitting somebody. I don't want to feel like this, dear Lord – but I do. Thank You for loving me as I am, not as I should be. Help me now to handle my feelings in a way that glorifies You and honours Your Name." When we pray a prayer like that – *and mean it* – we are on the way to maturity.

Facing and being willing to *feel* negative feelings such as grief, sorrow, hurt and emotional pain may not be something that excites us, but it is essential if we are to

know our Lord's purpose for our lives. When we are willing to go down into the hurt and feel it, then something glorious and transformative happens – we experience the loving comfort and compassion of our Lord. "Blessed are those who mourn, for *they will be comforted.*" Comforted? By whom? By the Triune God. He comes alongside us in our pain, and through the comfort He pours into our beings, enables us to become more sensitive to Him, to ourselves, and to others.

Isaiah 51:1–16 v. 12

After a lifetime of dealing with people and their problems, I have no hesitation in saying that the happiest people on earth are those who have been hurt but have had those hurts healed through the power of Christ's transforming love. They are what someone has called 'wounded healers'. Having been healed themselves, they go out to heal others. Going down into the pain of hurt feelings is not a very pleasant journey, but coming back from it with the comfort of God in your soul is an experience that is positively exhilarating and enriching. You return, not only with a new sensitivity in your soul, but with a new potential for ministering to others.

Remember this: great sorrow leads to great happiness – and without the sorrow, there can be no genuine happiness. This might sound to many like a contradiction in terms. It is not a contradiction, but a paradox – and a *blessed* one at that!

BLESSED ARE THE MEEK

We come now to Christ's third prescription for happiness: "Blessed are the meek, for they will inherit the earth." How we have shied away from that word 'meek'. We have thought of meekness as weakness and thus have a totally wrong concept of what Jesus meant. The Amplified Bible translates it thus: "Blessed are the meek (the mild, patient, long-suffering), for they shall inherit the earth."

The dictionary defines 'meek' as 'humble, compliant and submissive'. Does this mean that Jesus expects the children of the Kingdom to be like subdued puppies who crawl into their master's presence and cower at his feet? Or to become the type of people who lack inner fortitude and gumption, who can be easily pushed around and manipulated?

The truly *meek* person – in the Biblical sense of the word – is not timid, shy, hesitant and unassuming, but trusting, confident and secure. The root meaning of the word 'meekness' is that of yieldedness or surrender – a characteristic without which no real progress can be made in the Christian life. What happens, for example, to the scientist who approaches the mysteries of the universe in a manner that is aggressive and belligerent? He discovers nothing. But what happens to the scientist who approaches the mysteries of the universe in a spirit of meekness? He finds its richest secrets unfolding themselves to him and he is able to harness the mighty forces around him to advantage. The Christian who approaches life in the same spirit – the spirit of meekness and submission – discovers the true meaning of his existence and the purpose of God in all his affairs.

Psalm
149:1–9
v. 4

Now we must focus our thinking on the fact that the quality of meekness described in the Beatitudes is not the result of natural temperament, but comes from knowing Christ and abiding in Him. That goes, of course, for all the qualities enunciated in the Beatitudes – they are spiritual characteristics, not natural ones. This point needs elaborating, for there are many Christians who say: "I am aggressive by nature, so it is not possible for me to be a meek and mild person. This is how nature has endowed me and I must be the person I am."

1 Corinthians 6:1–11
v. 11

Every Christian, whatever their natural temperament, is meant to be like this. It is not a matter of natural disposition; it is a quality produced by the Spirit of God. Think of the powerful and extraordinary nature of a man like David – and yet observe his meekness. Look at a man like Paul the apostle, a master mind, a powerful and outstanding personality, yet consider his great humility and gentleness. How did these men get to be like this? Not because of a natural proneness towards meekness, but because they were indwelt by Christ and the Holy Spirit. It is not a matter of genes; it is a matter of grace.

Let us see what meekness is not. Firstly, meekness does not mean indolence. There are people who appear to be spiritually meek, but really they are not so at all – they are indolent. And this is not what Jesus is talking about in the Beatitudes. Again, meekness does not mean an easy-going type of attitude – the attitude seen in those who just take life as it comes. That is not meekness; that is flabbiness. There are some Christians who have such a casual air about them that one can easily mistake this for the quality which Jesus is referring to in the Beatitudes. We must learn to differentiate between that which is bestowed upon us by nature, and that which is bestowed upon us by grace.

Another thing that meekness ought not to be confused with is – niceness. There are people who are nice by nature. Dr Martyn Lloyd Jones says of such people: "Natural niceness is something biological, the kind of thing you get in animals. One dog is nicer than another, one cat nicer than another." Finally, meekness is not passivity, or a desire to obtain peace at any price. How often is the person regarded as meek who adopts

the attitude – anything is better than a disagreement.
This is the kind of passivity which does not make for
good mental or spiritual health. The most greatly used
men and women of God down the ages have been people
who were meek without being weak – strong men and
women, yet meek men and women. They were meek
enough to absorb the resources of God.

Now we can focus more precisely on what Jesus meant
when He said: "Blessed are the *meek*, for they will
inherit the earth." Meekness, as Jesus is using the word
here, refers to an attitude of heart and mind that is
entirely free from a spirit of demandingness and accepts
the will of God in its entirety.

I think J.B. Phillips gets close to the meaning in Jesus'
mind when he translates His statement thus: "Happy are
those who claim nothing, for the whole earth will belong
to them." I must stress once again that the thought here

1 Peter
3:1–12

v. 4

is not of passivity, but of active compliance and obedience to the will of God. "Meekness", said one commentator, "is essentially a true view of oneself, expressing itself in attitude and conduct with respect to others."

Colossians 3:1–15
v. 12

If that is so, then it means it is two things: (1) our attitudes toward ourselves, and (2) our attitudes toward others. The meek person is so sure of himself that he does not need to demand anything for himself. He does not see his rights as something to be rigidly held on to, but follows the spirit of Jesus as outlined in Philippians 2:6–7: "Who, although being essentially one with God ... did not think this equality with God was a thing to be eagerly grasped or retained; but stripped Himself of all privileges ... and was born a human being" (Amplified Bible).

Philippians 2:6–7

That is the place to which you and I must come if we

James

are to understand and practise the principle of
meekness. The Christian who is meek will not be over-
sensitive about himself, nor defensive; he realises that
he has no rights at all and delights to leave everything in
the hands of God. When he is called upon to suffer
unjustly, he remembers the word of the Lord that says:
"Vengeance is mine; I will repay", and trusts God to work
out the situation in His own time and in His own way. He
leaves himself and any cause in which he is involved in
God's hands, believing that as he adopts a quiet mind
and a meek spirit, the outcome will be the one which
God appoints. The poet Browning puts the same truth in
these words: "He who keeps one end in view makes all
things serve." When that one end is the purpose of God,
then indeed – all things serve.

3: 1–18
v. 13

What is there about this particular saying of Jesus
which engenders good mental health? Mental health,
after all, is more than a medical term. It is a concept that
goes beyond the walls of a hospital or a doctor's clinic
and applies also to the home, the church and the world
of everyday living.

Mental health is concerned with the dynamics of
relationship and adjustment – the way we handle such
things as anxiety, hostility and frustration. "Mental
health", says one authority, "concerns itself with the
everyday troubles of everyday people – helping them to
solve their problems or face them bravely when they
cannot be warded off." The statement of Jesus we are
focusing on at the moment contributes to good mental
health because it encourages us to be free from the
attitude of demandingness – the attitude that says:
"Things *must* go my way", "I *ought* to have some
consideration", "People *should* respect my rights."

One psychologist goes as far as to say that if we could eliminate the *shoulds* and *woulds* from our vocabulary and our inner attitudes, we could become transformed people overnight. He was not referring, of course, to the moral compass which God has placed within us that cries out for obedience to that which is right ("I *ought* not to lie", "I *should* always do right", etc.) but to the attitude of demandingness that insists on having one's rights irrespective of any other considerations. One of the biggest causes of mental and emotional illness is the attitude of demandingness and over-concern. Do we

wonder any longer why Christ congratulates the meek and promises them the earth?

Matthew 11:28–30

Let us now ask ourselves: what did Jesus mean by the phrase, *"for they will inherit the earth"*? It means, so I believe, that when we develop the attitude of meekness, the whole universe is behind us and throws itself on our side. If, for example, we decide to manifest the attitude of anger and hostility rather than cultivating a meek and quiet spirit, then the anger and hostility becomes, as someone put it, "sand in the machinery of life".

The universe is not designed to support such things as hatred, hostility or lies, for it has been made in a Christlike fashion. Paul, writing to the Colossians, shows that when God made the world, He made it to work in a certain way, and that way is the way of Christ: "All things were created through him (Christ) and for him." Edison,

Colossians 1:15–27 v. 16

the scientist, tried eleven hundred experiments, all of which turned out to be failures. Someone said to him: "You must feel that you have wasted your time." "Oh, no", said Edison, "I simply found out eleven hundred ways how not to do things."

This is what is happening in the world right now — humanity is finding out how to live. They are discovering that there are some things which the universe will not approve and some things it will approve. The meek are those who have come to terms with reality and know that they cannot twist it to their own ends or make it approve of what cannot be approved. Whoever has the first word in this universe must always remember that the universe has the last word. The Christian who adopts the attitudes of his Master finds the universe backing him in everything he does.

BLESSED ARE THOSE WHO HUNGER

We turn now to the next of our Lord's Beatitudes: "Blessed are those who hunger and thirst for righteousness, for they will be filled." One of the axioms of life is this – *everyone thirsts after something.* Some thirst for success, some thirst for fame, some thirst for stable relationships, and some thirst for financial security. But there is a thirst which is common to every human heart – the thirst for happiness. Notice, however, that Jesus does not say: "Happy are those who thirst for *happiness*", but "Happy are those who thirst for *righteousness*."

Matthew
6:19–34
v. 33

Happiness, therefore, is a by-product – to get it, you must focus on something else. We touched on this thought at the beginning of our study but now we must give it some further attention. Dr W. E. Sangster, the famous Methodist preacher, when dealing with this point in one of his sermons, put it like this: "Do you enjoy a game of golf or tennis? Then your pleasure is strictly proportioned to the degree to which you lose yourself in the game. While it lasts, it must absorb you: your whole mind should be on the game. If you stop in the midst of it and ask yourself precisely what degree of pleasure you are deriving from this particular stroke, the pleasure will evaporate and you will begin to feel rather foolish in following a wee white ball over a mile or two of turf."

To experience happiness, one must forget it and focus on something other than its pursuit. Those who reach out for happiness are forever unsatisfied – the more they strive, the less they find. Happiness, I say again, is a by-product; it is not something you find, but something that finds you.

Once again Jesus touches on an aspect of good mental health when He teaches us through these words to focus on right goals. Those who study human behaviour tell us that everything we do has a goal. "We are not conditioned animals that act automatically and unthinkingly in programmed response", says a psychologist, "... neither are we the hapless victims of internal forces that drive us relentlessly in unwanted directions." *Everything we do has a goal.* It may sometimes feel as if we do things we don't want to do, but the truth is that everything we do represents an effort to reach a goal that somehow, albeit at an unconscious level, makes sense. In fact, one of the ways in which you can better understand why you do the things you do is to ask yourself: what's my goal?

Colossians
1:1–14
v. 10

A woman I once counselled and who was extremely frustrated because her husband would not change to meet her requirements said to me: "My husband is so stubborn and obstinate that I just can't see any future for us together." I shared with her the concept that everything we do represents a goal, and asked her to put into words what she thought her goal might be in her marriage. Without a moment's hesitation she replied: "To change my husband." Her daily prayer was: "Lord, You love my husband and I'll change him." I suggested she altered her goal to: "Lord, You change my husband and I'll love him." She did, and instantly found a new freedom – and a new happiness in her marriage.

Permit me to differentiate between desires and goals. A goal is a purpose to which a person is unalterably committed and something for which he or she assumes unconditional responsibility. A desire is something *wanted* and which cannot be obtained without the co-operation of another human being. A desire must never become the motivating purpose behind our behaviour, for if it does, then it becomes a goal – and a goal that is likely to be blocked, causing negative emotions to arise and erupt within our being. Think of a man whose goal is to make money. Once he changes his goal to *pleasing the Lord* and then sees his concern to make money as merely a *desire* he will find instant release.

Keep in mind that what causes emotional problems to arise within us is invariably a blocked goal. Take another illustration that might help to make clearer the difference between goals and desires. Have you ever

found yourself talking to another Christian who seems to have difficulty in applying what seems to you a simple Biblical principle in their life? You point out the need to do as God says, but your friend fails to see the truth that to you is as clear as daylight. If you get frustrated at that point, the chances are that you are allowing a desire to become a goal. To *want* your friend to listen is a legitimate *desire,* but to get frustrated over it means you are *determined* to make him listen – and that becomes a goal.

If we make the obtaining of happiness a goal, it eludes us like a will-o'-the-wisp, but if we give up the chase and hold it only as a desire, then it comes home and takes up residence in our heart.

Let me repeat: there is nothing wrong in wanting to be happy; it is a natural and valid *desire* – but the paradoxical truth is that I will never be happy if I am primarily concerned with becoming happy. My overriding goal in every circumstance and situation must be to respond Biblically, to put the Lord and His righteousness first and seek to behave as He would want

me to. The wonderful truth is that as we devote our energies to the task of becoming what Christ wants us to be – righteous – He responds by filling us with unutterable happiness and joy. I must, therefore, firmly and consciously by an act of the will, refuse to make the obtaining of happiness my goal, and instead adopt the goal of becoming more like the Lord.

Hebrews
12:1–13
v. 2

An obsessive preoccupation with 'happiness' will obscure our understanding of the Biblical route to eternal peace and joy. And what is that route? Psalm 16:11: "At Your right hand there are pleasures for evermore." It follows that if we are to experience those

Psalm
16:11

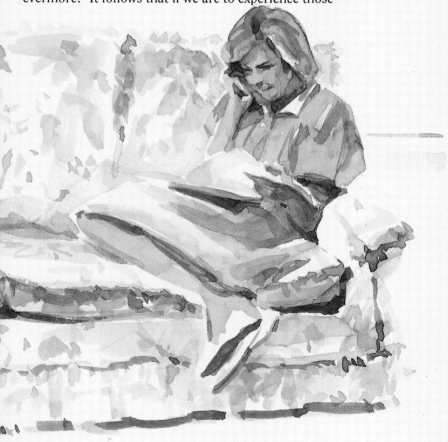

pleasures, then we must learn what it means to be at God's right hand. Paul tells us that Christ has been exalted to God's right hand (Eph. 1:20). Can anything be clearer? The more we abide in Christ, the more we shall experience true happiness.

Ephesians 1:20

There are still multiplied thousands of Christians paying no more than lip service to the truth that happiness is a by-product of righteousness. Happiness is their *goal*, righteousness merely their *desire*.

Now we ask ourselves: what happens to those who hunger and thirst after righteousness? The answer is clear: they will be filled. Make righteousness your goal

and you will be eternally satisfied. This fourth Beatitude carries us a step further in our understanding of Jesus' formulae for good spiritual and mental health. If I might venture upon a paraphrase of my own, I would put it like this: "Congratulations to those who ardently crave and desire to become more and more like me and to know my righteousness, for they shall find a satisfaction that will never vanish or be destroyed."

Philippians
3:7–21
v. 10

May I be permitted to ask you this personal question: what are you most hungering and thirsting for? Is it health? Is it relief from pain? Is it freedom from anxiety? Is it financial security? All of these are legitimate

cravings, but if your primary hunger and thirst is not to become more and more like Christ, then you will experience an inner emptiness that nothing can fill.

Let me point out one more thing – something that might astonish you – *to the extent that your deepest hunger and thirst are not toward God, to that extent will you experience spiritual and psychological problems.* If you are not hungering and thirsting after Him, you will hunger and thirst after something else. When we make it our goal to glorify God, then we will enjoy Him. We must not make it our goal to enjoy Him in order to glorify Him. Remember the goal of happiness is elusive, regardless of how well-thought-out is our strategy. But the by-product of happiness is freely available to those whose goal is to know God and be found in Him.

BLESSED ARE THE MERCIFUL

We come now to the fifth of Christ's famous sayings:
"Blessed are the merciful, for they will be shown mercy."
The true disciple of Jesus, according to our Lord,
manifests not just the characteristics we have previously
considered, but he is merciful also.

What does our Lord mean when He uses the word
'merciful'? The thought underlying the word is that of
compassion and concern for the plight of others. The
original word used in this fifth Beatitude is also used to
describe the High Priestly ministry of Christ in Hebrews
2:17. One authority, W.E. Vine, says that a 'merciful'
person is "not simply possessed of pity but is *actively*
compassionate".

Hebrews
2:17

It is important to stress once again that the
characteristic of being merciful of which our Lord spoke
here is not something that arises from our natural
temperament, but something that is bestowed on us
when we abide in Christ. As Dr Martyn Lloyd Jones says:
"This is not a gospel for certain temperaments – nobody
has an advantage over anybody else when they are face to
face with God." Again, mercy is not the turning of a blind
eye to moral violations – the attitude that pretends not
to see things. This can be seen most forcefully when we
consider that the term 'merciful' is an adjective which is
applied especially and specifically to God Himself. This
means that however the word applies to God, it applies
equally to man. God is merciful, but He is also truth:
"Mercy and truth are *met* together" (Psalm 85:10 AV). If
we think of mercy at the expense of truth and law, then it
is not true mercy; it is merely a caricature.

Psalm
85:10

One of the best ways to understand the word 'mercy'

is to compare it with grace. Have you ever noticed, when reading Paul's epistles, that in the introduction to every one of his epistles from Romans through to 2 Thessalonians, he uses the words: "Grace and peace to you from God our Father and the Lord Jesus Christ." The phrase usually appears in the second or third verse of every one of his epistles. However, when he comes to what are described as the pastoral epistles (1 and 2 Timothy and Titus), he changes the phrase to read: "Grace, *mercy* and peace from God the Father and Christ Jesus our Lord."

When Paul inserted the word 'mercy' after the word 'grace', he implied an interesting distinction. Someone has defined the two words thus: "Grace is especially associated with men in their sins; mercy is especially associated with men in their misery." While grace looks down upon sin and seeks to save, mercy looks especially upon the miserable *consequences* of sin and seeks to relieve. This helps us to see mercy in a wider dimension. *Mercy is compassion plus action.*

A Christian who is merciful feels such compassion and concern that he is not content until he does something about the plight of the one with whom he comes in contact. The story of the Good Samaritan is a classic illustration of being merciful. Others saw the man but did nothing to help him in his plight. The Samaritan, however, crossed the road, dressed the man's wounds, took him to an inn and made provision for his comfort. I say again: mercy is compassion *plus* action.

Someone has pointed out that the fifth Beatitude is

Luke 10:25–37
vv. 33–34

unique and quite different from the ones that precede it. In the first four, there is a contrast between the need and the fulfilment. The 'poor in spirit' receive the kingdom; those 'who mourn' are comforted; 'the meek' inherit the earth; those who 'hunger and thirst' are satisfied; but in the fifth Beatitude, the theme changes – 'the *merciful* will be shown *mercy*'. It is as though we cannot receive mercy without first giving it.

We must move carefully here, for no Beatitude has been more misunderstood than this one. There are those who take these words to mean that we can only be forgiven by God to the extent that we forgive others. They bring alongside this Beatitude such passages as: "Forgive us our sins, for we also forgive everyone who sins against us" (Luke 11:4), and "This is how my heavenly Father will treat each of you unless you forgive your brother from your heart" (Matt.18:35).

Luke 11:4
Matthew 18:35

Putting all these Scriptures together, they claim that it is the clear meaning of the Bible that we are forgiven by God only to the extent that we forgive others. If this is so, then salvation is by works and not by grace. We must never interpret Scripture in a way that contradicts other Scriptures. What our Lord means in this fifth Beatitude is that when we demonstrate mercy to others, we make it possible for God's mercy to penetrate deeper into our own lives and personalities. The act of giving makes us more able to receive.

Luke 6:27–40
v. 38

Since we are saved by grace, through faith, what is Scripture getting at when it seems to encourage us to forgive in order that we might be forgiven? I think it refers to the matter of *realised* forgiveness.

I know many Christians, as I am sure you do, who, although they have been forgiven by God, are never really sure of it. And one of the major reasons for this is that they have never taken the steps to get rid of the bitterness and resentment they hold in their hearts toward others. The problem they experience in not *feeling* forgiven is not God's fault, but their own. He has forgiven them on the basis of their own personal repentance, but His forgiveness is unable to reach the centre of their spirit and dissolve their feelings of guilt because they harbour an unforgiving attitude toward others.

Ephesians 4:17–32
v. 32

How does this fifth Beatitude, when practised, engender within us good mental and spiritual health? Psychologists have shown that those who lack the qualities of mercy and compassion in their disposition

are more likely to develop physical problems than any other group of people. Harsh, judgmental attitudes may bring a sense of satisfaction to the person who does not know the meaning of mercy, but it is a false sense of satisfaction. Our human constitution is not made to function effectively on any attitude that is foreign to the spirit of Jesus Christ.

A Christian doctor says: "We are allergic to wrong attitudes just as some people are allergic to shrimps." I am physically allergic to red and green peppers. I have tried them scores of times, but it always has the same result – I get sick. I am just as allergic to harsh, judgmental attitudes. I can't assimilate them. They disrupt me – body, soul and spirit. And what goes for me goes also for you. When we fail to practise the principles which our Lord outlined for us in the Beatitudes, then our sense of well-being is lowered, depleted and poisoned. Goodness is good for us – spiritually, mentally and physically.

What would happen if we really put into practice this important attitude and principle? It would mean that we would look at everyone through Christian eyes. We would see sinners, not merely as the dupes and victims of sin and Satan, but as men and women who are to be *pitied*. We would see a fellow Christian who falls by the way, not as someone to be clobbered, but as someone to be lifted.

Far too many of us in the Christian Church walk about with judgmental attitudes, and whenever anyone slips up, we either bang them over the head with a Bible text or wither them with a look of scorn. We have the philosophy of an eye for an eye and a tooth for a tooth. Failure is met with derision and wrong is met with

Philippians
2:1–11
v. 4

contempt. I have no hesitation in saying that such attitudes ought not to be found among the people of God. Wherever they are present, they will eat like acid into the soul. Being merciful means letting Christ have control of our lives so that His gentleness overcomes our vindictiveness, His kindness our unkindness, and His bigness our littleness.

Are you a merciful person? Do you look upon those who have fallen with concern and compassion – or is your attitude one of contempt, derision and scorn? Can you feel pity for those who have been duped by the world, the flesh and the devil? If so, then – congratulations! You have passed the test and are on your way to experiencing spiritual health and happiness. Blessed indeed are those who are merciful – for they shall obtain mercy.

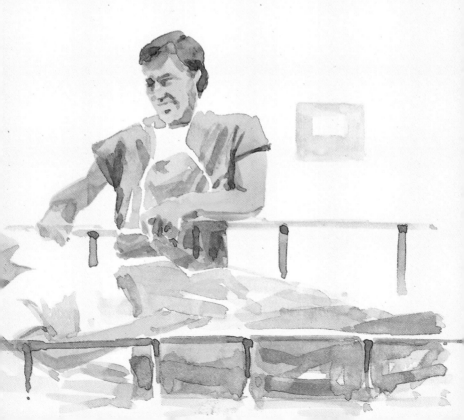

BLESSED ARE THE PURE IN HEART

Next we come to the Beatitude which is considered by many commentators to be the most sublime of them all: "Blessed are the pure in heart, for they will see God."

We begin by asking ourselves: what is meant by the term 'heart'? According to the general use of the word in Scripture, it has reference to what goes on in the core of our being. It means more than just the seat of the affections and emotions; it is the fount from which everything proceeds. Jesus told His disciples: "Out of the heart come evil thoughts, murder, adultery, sexual immorality..." and so on. Dr Oswald Chambers says: "If a sinner really wishes to understand his heart, then let him listen to his own mouth in an unguarded frame for five minutes."

Matthew
15:1–20
v. 19

Someone has pointed out that the gospel of Jesus Christ is a religion of *new* things. It offers to men a *new* birth, a *new* life, a *new* hope, a *new* happiness – and, at the end of time – a *new* name. However, out of all these fascinating *new* things which Christ offers His children, none is perhaps more intriguing than His offer of a new heart. The promise is first given in the prophecy of Ezekiel: "A new heart I will give you, and a new spirit I will put within you" (Ezek. 36:26, RSV). Quite clearly, when it comes to spiritual things, the heart of the matter is the matter of the heart. Christ's offer of changing our hearts is, without doubt, one of the greatest promises of the Bible. Be encouraged – our Lord is not content with tinkering about on the surface of our lives – His goal is to purify our *hearts*.

Ezekiel
36:26

When we understand what Scripture means by the term 'heart' we can ask ourselves another important question: what does our Lord mean when He uses the word 'pure'? "Blessed are the *pure* in heart, for they will see God."

The word 'pure' (Greek: *katharos*) means a heart that Acts 15:1–11 v. 9 is *clean* or *clear*. Unfortunately, *purity* does not seem to be a popular word in contemporary Christianity. The emphasis nowadays seems to be more on *power* than purity. Most Christians I talk to want to know how they can possess and develop spiritual gifts. Few, generally speaking, want to know how to experience the blessing of what our text today calls a heart *purified* by faith. Someone has said of modern-day Christians that they "long to be good the easy way". The attitude of many toward the subject of purity can be summed up in the couplet:

> *"Won't somebody give me some good advice*
> *On how to be naughty – and still be nice."*

Nearly sixteen hundred years ago St Augustine expressed the same thought in words which might well contain the thoughts of many – thankfully, not all – in today's Church: "Lord, make me pure ... but not just yet." Most of us would be willing to identify ourselves with the conditions laid down in the first five of our Lord's Beatitudes, but how do we feel about the condition of being *pure* in heart?

Great controversy has raged around this issue in Psalm 51:1–15 v. 10 every century of the Christian Church. Those who see sin as having made deep inroads into human nature say that the only thing God can do with sin is to forgive it. Others see the soul as a battleground on which a long-drawn-out guerilla warfare takes place between the flesh and the Spirit. And there are those who claim, as did John Wesley, that inner purity can be imparted by a sudden influx of divine grace.

These three main views in the Church can be presented in this way: (1) those who believe that purity is imputed; (2) those who believe that purity is imparted; and (3) those who believe that purity is developed. Those who believe purity is *imputed* say that Christ flings His robe of righteousness around a sinner and then God forever sees him in the spotless garments of His Son. Those who believe purity is *imparted* claim that there is an experience awaiting all believers, usually subsequent

to conversion, whereby, through a crisis experience, God imparts the gift of purity. This belief received great prominence under John Wesley. Those who believe purity is *developed* see the work of God in the soul proceeding along the lines of a slow but steady improvement.

Which of these is right? I believe that each view has something to contribute: it is when the emphasis is disproportionately placed that problems arise. God both imputes and imparts purity, and then helps us apply and develop these truths in our daily life and experience.

The word 'catharsis' – meaning to cleanse or make

pure – is derived from the same Greek root as the word 'pure'.

In psychology, the word 'catharsis' is used to describe the feeling of release and cleansing a person experiences in the presence of a trusted friend or counsellor when they empty out a lot of repressed feelings or ideas. In the right circumstances and under the right conditions, a person who does this often feels purged, renewed and released. I have seen this happen myself on countless occasions when counselling. A person comes with deep hurts, and when they are sure they are in the presence of someone who understands them, someone they can

trust, they open up their repressed feelings in such a way that afterwards they sit back and say, "I feel so different. It's like someone has reached deep down inside me and scraped my insides clean."

What produces this feeling of purging and release? It is difficult to explain because the inner release they feel is not obtained simply by sharing – *it comes only in the atmosphere of mutual confidence and trust.* When a counsellor shows signs of disapproval or shock, then no deep release (catharsis) is experienced. If, as mental health experts claim, this only happens when a counsellor is warm and accepting, as opposed to harsh and judgmental, then it becomes immediately obvious that in the presence of Jesus, the *Wonderful Counsellor,*   Isaiah we have the possibility of experiencing the deepest   9:1–7 catharsis it is possible to know.   v. 6

We cannot understand the sixth Beatitude unless we understand the phrase: "Blessed are the pure in heart, *for they will see God.*" The concluding words of this Beatitude are often misunderstood. Many believe it to have reference to the saints' eternal reward in heaven. Tennyson expressed this thought in his famous lines:

> *"I hope to see my Pilot face to face*
> *When I have crossed the bar."*

The thought contained in this phrase, however, is not   Psalm so much related to seeing God in heaven, but in seeing   24: 1–10 God *now*. Seeing God means seeing God in everything.   v. 3 Let me put it another way: not to see God is to fail to find the meaning of life and to see no purpose in anything. Such a condition, one must admit, produces an emotional overload on the personality that leads inevitably to despair. Some who fall prey to this mood end up committing suicide. As someone put it: "Those who can't see the *why* have little energy to cope with the *what*."

Seeing God is being acquainted with Him, sensing His acceptance, comprehending what it means to be forgiven and made anew. Raymond Cramer puts it beautifully when he says: "To the pure in heart, seeing God is viewing a stained glass window from the inside rather than the outside. The pure in heart are aware of a reality which most people miss. *They are sure of God.*" Seeing God must irrevocably be connected with purity of heart, for we must see and sense God first in our own inner being before we can see Him and sense Him elsewhere. See Him within and you will not fail to see Him without.

BLESSED ARE THE PEACEMAKERS

We come now to the seventh positive attitude that
makes for good spiritual and mental health: "Blessed are
the peacemakers, for they will be called sons of God."
This Beatitude seems to have a special relevance to the
age through which we are passing, for if there is one
thing the world needs at this moment, it is –
peacemakers.

Our generation has never known peace on a
worldwide basis. One authority says: "During most of
recent history the air has been filled with rumblings of
pending war until today, at the so-called peak of
scientific enlightenment, the menace of global conflict

threatens our atomic age with suicide." The uncertainty of being constantly on the brink of nuclear confrontation is taking its toll on the people of all nations, spiritually and psychologically. Studies show that living in a generation which has the power to annihilate itself in global destruction has a crippling effect upon the minds of thousands, if not millions of people.

There was never a time when peacemakers were as important as they are now. And more and more are standing up to be counted on the side of peace. The peace organisations report increasing memberships and their attempts to alert the world to the need for international treaties continues to gain the attention of

every section of the media. Yet how strange that most of those who are so concerned for peace between nations fail to see the need for peace between themselves and their Creator. The solemn truth is that no man or woman can become a peacemaker – at least in the Biblical sense of the word – until they have found peace within their innermost being.

Romans 5:1–11 v. 1

As we are looking at the Beatitudes from the point of view of how effective they are in producing good spiritual and mental health, it is interesting to see how the psychology of Jesus is always ahead of the findings of those who study human behaviour. The view of many psychologists and psychiatrists is that much of the talk and activity by the masses in relation to international peace is actually a projection whereby they take the pressure off themselves. I am not convinced that all the concern can be dismissed in this way, but a lot of it can be explained in terms of the mechanism known as psychological projection.

Listen to what Louis Linn and Leo Schwartz say in their book *Psychiatry, Religion and Experience:* "A psychological origin of an adolescent's social idealism lies in his yearning for peace within himself. He tends to project his feelings of helplessness and turmoil on to the outer world, so that his yearning for peace may take the form of a wish for world peace." Many of the activists who work for world peace may find this difficult to accept, but the truth is that if they did not have a world crisis on which to project their feelings, they would have to create some other condition. As long as we are not at peace within ourselves, we will create situations on which we project our insecure feelings.

Psalm 139:1–24 v. 23

I hasten to say that not everyone who is involved in

peace movements is motivated by this reason. I know a number of genuine Christians – people who already have the peace of God in their hearts – who are active in the peace organisations and have a genuine concern to bring pressure on world governments to do everything that must be done to avoid the horrors of nuclear war. Nevertheless, I have no hesitation in saying that the majority of those involved in the peace organisations are motivated by this strange mechanism – projection. Since they do not possess peace within themselves, they talk at length about international peace.

Isaiah
48:12–22
v. 22

It is easier to blame the world leaders, the political parties, the Presidents and Prime Ministers than to look into one's own heart and accept individual

accountability. Actually the reason why there is so much war and hostility in the world is because, generally speaking, we do not possess peace within ourselves. We create an environment that reflects our inner conflicts – the outside world reflects our inner world. Peace between nations does not guarantee peace within nations, nor does peace between two people guarantee peace within an individual.

The Bible is not content to leave the nature of the peace Christ purchased for us in doubt. The Bible tells us that Christ made peace by the blood of His cross (Eph. 2:14). He bore the sins of men so that those who know Him and accept His meritorious sufferings on the cross

Ephesians 2:11–22

v. 14

need no longer be troubled by them. The greatest message the world has ever heard – or will ever hear – is this: Christ interposed Himself between sinful humanity and a holy God so that men and women could be eternally redeemed. Have you been redeemed? Have you accepted Christ's sacrifice for you on the cross? If so, good – your mission now in life is to be a peacemaker. You are to share His peace with others.

A little girl who, a few weeks earlier, had become a Christian came down from her bedroom one morning and said to her mother: "What a beautiful day." The surprised mother said: "What do you mean? It's raining like I've never seen it rain before, and the weather

forecast is that we are going to have several more days of this. How can you call such weather beautiful?" "But mother," the little girl replied, "a beautiful day has nothing to do with the weather." In those simple but powerful words, she reconciled her mother to the weather – and had a more beautiful day herself. You see, this is what peacemaking is all about. The peacemakers make a new world around them and within them.

A psychiatrist was interviewing a man full of conflicts. In the middle of the interview the telephone rang, and because the receptionist had put a call through to him when he had given instructions not to be disturbed, the psychiatrist swore. He lost his peace and he lost his patient. For the patient saw that he had little to give except verbal advice.

The fact is that when we lose our peace with others, it is usually the projection of an inner conflict within ourselves. The one who is constantly out of patience with the family or the people with whom he works is usually out of patience with himself. A church in the Far East has this statement engraved over the door: "Let James 3:1–18 v. 18 every Christian begin the work of union within himself." This is the place to begin – within yourself. For, as the Chinese saying puts it: "He who has peace in himself has peace in the family; he who has peace in the family has peace in the world."

We can even affirm that no one can be spiritually or mentally healthy until they know what it means to have peace in their inner beings. A psychologist says: "If we could only measure the amount of emotional energy that is dissipated within the human personality by lack of peace, we would be surprised to find that physical, mental and emotional loss would represent our greatest deficit within the human economy." He is simply saying that inner conflict tears us apart – physically, mentally and spiritually.

The intriguing thing is that as we make peace with God, a change comes into our own lives and this, in turn, is reflected in the lives of other people. We are not only at peace – we become peaceable. But even more – we become peacemakers. To be a peacemaker means, quite simply, that we become reconcilers. We reconcile people to God and to each other.

We should be careful not to misunderstand the meaning of the word 'peacemaker', so let's examine for a moment what it is not. Peacemaking is not just keeping

the peace. Some strive to keep the peace because they do not wish to risk any unpleasantness that might be involved in trying to put matters right. They avoid a conflict by smoothing over the surface, but this is not peace. The true peacemaker sometimes has to be a fighter. Paradoxically, he or she is called, not to a passive life, but an active one. Peacemaking, at times, can be exceedingly difficult – especially within the Christian Church. Those who pursue this ministry must realise that peacemaking is not patching things up, but getting to the roots of the problem. Peacemakers sometimes have to stir up trouble before they can resolve it.

Titus
2:1–15
v. 15

Peacemaking is a positive attitude and the one who has this attitude, according to Jesus, is to be envied and congratulated. The promise of the seventh Beatitude is that peacemakers "will be called sons of God." Why *called*? Because they *are* sons of God. This is their lot in life. "Sons are those who in character and life resemble God in closest similarity." Dr Martyn Lloyd Jones puts it like this: "The meaning of being called the sons of God is that the peacemaker is a child of God *and that he is like his Father."*

1 John
2:28—3:11
3:1

If I were to pick out the one verse that most perfectly expresses the meaning of the Christian Gospel, it would be this: "God was in Christ reconciling the world to himself ... and entrusting to us the message of reconciliation" (2 Cor. 5:19, RSV). Ever since man sinned, God has been engaged in the positive business of an outgoing love – seeking to reconcile those who did not want to be reconciled. God wants us to do what He does – He commits to us the same word of reconciliation. This attitude enables us to live life to the full – a life free from mental, emotional and spiritual problems.

2 Corinthians
5:19

Those who are inwardly reconciled to God and seek to reconcile others to Him and to each other will never suffer from psychological problems. They are the healthiest and the happiest people on earth. In two outstanding passages in the Bible, we are called sons of the Father – and for the same reason: Matthew 5:9 and Matthew 5:45. What do we conclude from this? We are most like God when we are bringing people together in reconciliation. And those who try to reconcile others are doing the work of heaven – for it is heaven's work to reconcile us.

Matthew
5:9, 45

BLESSED ARE THOSE PERSECUTED ...

We come now to Christ's eighth and final prescription
for good spiritual and mental health: "Blessed are those
who are persecuted because of righteousness, for theirs
is the kingdom of heaven." The inevitable result of
bringing our attitudes in line with Christ's attitudes is
that our lives become a silent judgment upon others.
And men and women do not like to be judged, so they
kick back in persecution. "Society", said someone,
"demands conformity: if you fall beneath its standards, it
will punish you: if you rise above its standards, it will
persecute you. It demands an average, grey conformity."

The true Christian, however, does not conform – he
stands out. His head is lifted so high above the
multitudes that, not surprisingly, he gets hit. "Woe to
you", said Jesus, "when all men speak well of you" (Luke
6:26, NIV). If they do speak well of us, then it could be
that we are too much like them. Let there be no mistake
about this, the righteous will be persecuted – inevitably
so. Once we adopt the attitudes and principles which
Christ presents so clearly for us in His Sermon on the
Mount, the men and women of the world are going to
react with hostility and indignation.

Many Christians find great difficulty in coming to
terms with this issue of persecution, and because they
have never understood that those who reject Christ will
also reject those who follow Christ, they become
entangled in such things as conciliation and
compromise.

If you have never done so before, face the fact right
now that when you identify yourself with Jesus Christ,
the world will persecute you. The degree of persecution

Luke 6:26

Philippians
1:12–30
v. 29

2 Timothy
3:12–17
v. 12

differs from one Christian to another, but always remember that a close relationship with Jesus Christ will cause the world, in one way or another, to react against you with hostility and contempt. Once you face this fact, you are nine-tenths of the way toward overcoming the fear which cripples so many Christians – the fear of witnessing.

Not long after my conversion to Christ, an old Welsh miner gave me some advice that greatly helped to overcome my fear of rejection. He said: "Keep ever before you the fact that those who reject Christ will reject you. And the more like Christ you become, the more the world will resent you. Remember also that

when they do reject you, it is not you personally whom they are against, but Christ who is alive and who is being seen in you." Never shall I forget the release that came to me through those wise words. Once I understood that becoming identified with Christ meant I was on a collision course with the world, I came to terms with the inevitability of this fact and was set free from fear. And what happened to me can happen to you – today.

Many Christians are ineffective witnesses because they attempt to water down their testimony so as to avoid misunderstanding or persecution – and they end up achieving nothing. Once we understand and accept the fact that those who reject Christ and His principles will also reject us, we will then be free to throw our whole weight on the side of Christ and become fully identified with Him.

In following this principle, however, we must be careful that our freedom from fear of rejection or persecution does not lead us to become objectionable. I know some Christians who have a hard time from their non-Christian acquaintances, not because of their likeness to Christ, but because of their tactlessness and lack of wisdom. I once knew a man who told me he had convincing evidence that he was a true disciple of Christ. I was intrigued to know his reason for thinking this way, and in answer to my question: "Why are you so sure?" he replied: "My neighbours won't talk to me and cross to the other side of the road when they see me coming. I take this persecution as proof that I am a true citizen of the kingdom."

Some time later, I had occasion to talk to some of this man's neighbours, who told me that the reason they avoided him was because he continually accosted them

Matthew
10:1–20
v. 16

with questions like: "Do you know you are going to hell?" or "What if you were to drop dead at this moment – where would you spend eternity?" The neighbours thought it good policy to avoid him rather than to be faced continually with his belligerence. The man was suffering, not for Christ's sake, but for his own sake.

This eighth Beatitude – "Blessed are those who are persecuted because of righteousness, for theirs is the kingdom of heaven" – does not apply to people who are persecuted because of tactlessness and folly. Let us be quite clear about that.

1 Peter 4:7–19

v. 15

There is a great difference between being persecuted for the sake of righteousness and being persecuted for the sake of self-righteousness. Many Christians are foolish in these matters. They fail to realise the difference between prejudice and principle, and thus bring unnecessary suffering upon themselves. The same applies to those who are over-zealous in their witnessing. They make a nuisance of themselves and interpret the persecution that comes as a result as persecution for righteousness' sake.

The Scripture teaches us to be "wise as serpents and innocent as doves". The writer of the Proverbs puts it powerfully when he says: "He who wins souls is wise." We are not told in this eighth Beatitude, "Blessed are those who are persecuted because they are over-zealous", neither are we told, "Blessed are those who are persecuted because they are fanatical." I was once asked by a church to counsel one of their members who had a compulsion to witness. The man got into so many difficulties because of this that the church threatened to discipline him unless he agreed to receive counselling. I found his compulsion to witness came not from Christ, but from his own inner drives. He *needed* to witness so as to feel significant. Witnessing should be a constraint, never a compulsion.

I want to take this matter a stage further, and suggest that in relation to this matter of suffering and persecution, some Christians have developed a 'martyr complex'.

A 'martyr complex' is an attitude of mind that finds some strange emotional satisfaction in being persecuted. Why should this be? Well, if, for example, a person does not experience a good sense of personal worth, they become motivated to secure that worth in other ways. And one of those ways can be that of making an impact upon their immediate environment or society through taking a stand on some 'Christian' issue.

Now I am not saying, of course, that all of those who take a stand on such issues as pornography, violence, and other serious moral problems in our nation are motivated to do so because of a 'martyr complex'. That would be foolish to suggest and foolish to deduce. But it must be seen that some Christians strike out on issues, not because of an overriding concern for Christian values, but because of the satisfaction they get out of being noticed. And when being noticed leads to severe persecution, they draw from this the emotional charge they need to compensate for their low sense of worth. Such people almost court suffering and persecution, but it has to be said that they are not suffering for righteousness' sake – they are suffering for their own sake. May God give us grace and wisdom to understand when we are doing things to meet our own emotional needs, rather than out of love for Him.

Some feel that the verses which follow this Beatitude (verses 11 & 12) constitute a ninth Beatitude, but really they are an amplification and enlargement of what our Lord has been saying in verse 10. It must be pointed out in passing that more is said about this eighth Beatitude than is said about the others – a fact that surely underlines its supreme importance.

Matthew
5:11, 12

One question we must ask ourselves is this: how does

this eighth Beatitude contribute to good mental and spiritual health? It does so by encouraging us to stand up and be counted. The famous missionary doctor and scientist Dr Albert Schweitzer, when addressing a group of medical men in Africa many years ago, is reported to have said: "You cannot be healthy unless you *stand* for something – even at a cost."

The person who unashamedly identifies with Christ and stands up for Him, knowing that their stand will produce, in one form or another, inevitable persecution experiences an inner release from fear that affects every part of the personality in the most positive way. The

Deuteronomy
30:1–20
v. 19

positive may be persecuted, but they are also the most productive – they survive when others fall by the way. So stop wearing out your nervous system. Cease using up precious energy trying to find ways to make it through this world. Follow God's blueprint as laid out in the eight Beatitudes and yours will be a life which, through the psychology of Jesus, will bring you maximum effectiveness with minimum weariness. Choose any other way and you will experience minimum effectiveness with maximum weariness. I choose *life*.

Let us now take a simple test. Ask yourself the following questions and see how many of Christ's 'beautiful attitudes' have been assimilated into your life:

1. *Am I trying to grasp things from God's hands or are my hands relaxed and empty so that I might receive?*
2. *Do I shrink from painful experiences or do I welcome them in the knowledge that they will make me a more sensitive person?*
3. *Am I so sure of God and His resources that I am free from a spirit of demandingness and over-concern?*
4. *Is my goal to be happy, or is it to be holy? Am I more taken up with getting pleasure out of God than I am with giving pleasure to God?*
5. *Do I have a deep compassion and concern for the plight of others?*
6. *Is my heart clean and pure? Have I experienced an inner cleansing that has reached to the deepest depths?*
7. *Am I a reconciler – one who seeks to reconcile others to God and, where necessary, to each other?*
8. *Am I so identified with Christ that I experience the hatred which the world gives to those who remind them of Him?*

Don't be discouraged if you can't see all of these 'beautiful attitudes' at work in your life. Remember, we *grow* in grace. Ask God, however, to help you absorb more and more of His 'beautiful attitudes' day by day. The more you have, the more you are to be envied. Possess them all – and you are truly *blessed*.